THE
LITTLE TEA
BOOK

Isha Mellor

PIATKUS

Other titles in the series

The Little Green Avocado Book
The Little Garlic Book
The Little Pepper Book
The Little Lemon Book
The Little Apple Book
The Little Strawberry Book
The Little Mushroom Book
The Little Nut Book
The Little Bean Book
The Little Honey Book
The Little Mustard Book
The Little Rice Book
The Little Coffee Book

© 1985 Judy Piatkus (Publishers) Limited

British Library Cataloguing in Publication Data

Mellor, Isha
    The little tea book.
    1. Tea
    I. Title
    641.3'372   TX415
    ISBN 0-86188-339-X

Drawings by Linda Broad
Designed by Ken Leeder
Cover illustrated by Lynne Robinson

Typeset by Phoenix Photosetting, Chatham
Printed and bound by The Bath Press, Avon

CONTENTS

'I'M DYING FOR A CUPPA!'

There is no need in Britain to explain that the exhausted speaker is referring to a cup of tea. Tea is the reviver of flagging spirits, the solace of the downcast, the excuse for a break, and usually the first refreshment offered to a newcomer. What is the virtue of this beverage? How did it arrive on our shores? Who first drank it? And how much do we drink in a year? A study of the history of tea and its place in our lives will surely produce more respect for that ritual cuppa.

THE TEA PLANT

The tea plant is one of the Camellia family (*Camellia sinensis*). The leaves are stiff, shiny and pointed, and the flowers, which resemble the buttercup in shape, are white with golden stamens. The plant requires an acid soil and a warm, wet climate with at least 50 inches of rain a year. It grows at varying altitudes up to 7,000 feet, and depending on the variety can have an economic life of between 40 and 100 years.

China is credited with originating tea cultivation, and tea plants now grow in about 30 countries, from Georgia in the Soviet Union and Turkey to South Africa and South America. The natural habitat of the tea plant is the triangular area reaching from the India–Burma border in the west, across China to the east, and south through Burma and Thailand into Vietnam.

Left to itself a tea plant would grow to 50 feet in height, so it is trained and pruned to produce a bush of about waist height to make for easy plucking by hand. Continual pruning and feeding result in large quantities of young shoots ready for plucking every seven to 14 days.

Most new bushes are grown from cuttings which need three to five years to develop and become ready for harvesting. The cuttings are cared for in nurseries, protected from the strong sun by bamboo shades.

In some countries the crop is seasonal and in others, such as Kenya, harvesting can continue through most of the year. In Sri Lanka the season lasts for six months, but at different times according to which side of the island the plantations are situated. India, being so vast and with varying climates, has several different harvesting times.

The quality of tea depends on climatic conditions. At higher altitudes the growth of the plants is slower and the crops smaller, but the quality will be superior.

Girls are generally employed as pickers because of their nimble fingers. They pluck the bud and two top leaves from each stalk and collect them in baskets carried on their backs. Because they work waist high in the dense plantations, the harvesters in India and Sri Lanka wear a kind of plastic apron to protect their saris. The rows are only two feet apart, and the plants are staggered at four feet intervals. The plucking has to be done fast for the leaves wither quickly. Harvesting is carried out about once a week.

Attempts to mechanize harvesting have never matched the skill of human pluckers who can gather 60 to 80 pounds (30–35 kilos) in a day, which is enough to make between 17 and 20 pounds (7½–9 kilos) of manufactured tea.

At The Tea Factory

T he freshly gathered shoots are taken to the factory, which is sited on the tea estate, or tea garden as it is often called. The complete manufacturing process produces the tea which is known as black tea. Black tea makes up 98 per cent of the international tea trade and is the familiar amber-coloured tea, full-flavoured and without any bitterness. Green tea does not go through the fermenting process and the leaves are heated (roasted in an iron pan or steamed) to prevent fermentation. It makes a pale greenish-yellow tea, mild but slightly bitter and much favoured by the Chinese. Oolong tea lies somewhere between black and green teas, slightly bitter and a light brownish-green colour.

Withering: The leaves are spread on racks in a current of warm dry air to remove moisture and render them limp and ready for the next stage.

Rolling: Natural juices and enzymes are released by crushing, tearing, and rolling through machines.

Fermentation: A truer term for this would be oxydization, during which the leaves are spread on scrupulously clean tables in a cool and humid atmosphere in which they turn a bright copper colour after about three hours.

Drying: The fermented leaves are then dried on trays which move slowly through hot air chambers until the leaves turn black.

Sorting: The leaves are finally sorted into different grades (or sizes) by sifting machines which vibrate them through different sized meshes.

Packing: The tea is packed into plywood chests lined with paper and foil. The tea chests are loaded on to pallets, 20 at a time, and shipped to their destinations.

It takes about 24 hours for a batch of tea to go through all these processes to the packaging stage. The determining factor is the varying time that withering can take. After each batch, the floors, walls and ceilings of the factory and the machinery are thoroughly washed in order to prevent any contamination for the following batch.

'There is a great deal of poetry and fine sentiment in a chest of tea.'

Ralph Waldo Emerson (1803–82)

GRADING TEA

In the final sorting or grading, tea acquires the colourful names that are used in the trade. They do not refer to quality but to the size and appearance of the tea. There are two main grades – leaf and broken leaf.

Leaf grades: These have the larger leaves and are classified as Orange Pekoe and Pekoe.

Broken leaf grades: Broken Orange Pekoe and Broken Pekoe.

In the terminology of tea, *Pekoe* is Chinese for leaf, and *Orange* is the colour of the tea bud when dried.

Within the broken leaf type there are further divisions which include:

Fannings: All small leaf teas, which include B.O.P. Fannings, Pekoe Fannings, and Fannings.

Dust: This unfortunate term is given to the smallest leaf particle size and is certainly not 'dust from the factory floor' as some like to say. What is found on the floor is known as dirt and is swept up to be used as fertilizer on the tea estates.

Brokens and Fannings give a darker liquor than the leaf grades, which yield more flavour and fragrance.

Tea is not only drunk. In Burma, Thailand and China, pickled tea leaves are eaten as a vegetable called *leppet-so.*

COUNTRIES OF ORIGIN

T ea is imported into the United Kingdom from about 25 different countries, the bulk coming from India.

India (35%)
Kenya (18%)
Sri Lanka (10.3%)
Malawi (6.5%)
Mozambique (4.3%)
Tanzania (3.5%)
China/Taiwan (3.4%)

Indonesia (3.1%)
Bangladesh (2.6%)
Others, including
USSR, Turkey,
Uganda, Zaire, Mauri-
tius, Brazil, Ecuador,
Papua/New Guinea

Britain imports annually about 200,000 metric tonnes, consumes some 170,000, and then re-exports worldwide a balance of 30,000 as selected packet teas. 12,000 tonnes go to Europe, for example, 3,861 to Canada, 2,218 to the United States, and 500 to Australia.

HOW MUCH TEA DO WE DRINK?

In the United Kingdom, every man, woman and child over 10 drinks approximately four cups of tea a day, coming second to the people of Eire who are the highest consumers in the world. India is the largest producer of tea and manages to drink half of what it produces.

TEA AUCTIONS

T ea deteriorates and cannot be stored for more than a few months. This, combined with fluctuating supply and demand, has caused several price slumps over the years, the most serious being in 1886, 1879, 1920, 1932, 1952 and 1970. After the 1932 slump an International Tea Committee was established by three of the producing countries – India, Ceylon and the Dutch East Indies (Indonesia) – to stabilize demand. Subsequent slumps have been caused by considerably increased production by other tea growing countries.

When the chests of tea arrive in Britain, they are sold at public auction. The first such auction was held in London in 1834, and there are now auctions in Calcutta, Colombo, Cochin, Chittagong and Nairobi, dealing in the teas from their particular areas.

The centre for the tea trade moved from Mincing Lane in London to Sir John Lyon House near St Paul's cathedral in 1971. Sales are held on Mondays, and deal in teas from about 25 countries. Bidding is based on details supplied by a tea taster. The auctioneer acts for the growers, and the buyers act through brokers.

The name 'tea' comes from the Chinese word *t'e* which is pronounced *tay*, and in Cantonese dialect as *tcha*. Via India we get the familiar word *cha*.

TEA TASTING

It can take five years to train a palate capable of tasting one to 300 teas in a day. Mistakenly, people imagine that a tea taster drinks the liquid until he is awash with it, but, as in the case of wine tasting, this is not so.

The taster is presented with identical amounts of infused liquid, which is poured into a handle-less cup. The infused leaf is tipped on to the inside of the tea pot lid for examination, and there is also an example of the dry leaf. The taster will note the appearance of the tea, its taste and flavour, and the appearance and aroma of the dry and the infused leaves. He is looking for a leaf which is dry and hard, well rolled and shiny. When infused, the quality is indicated by a bright copper coloured leaf, and the liquor should also be bright, with an aroma. The language of tasters uses words like malty, pungent, and brisk. There are about 120 different terms which can be used.

Each batch of tea must be exactly the same – in tea leaf weight, in the amount of boiling water used, in the equipment, and in the infusion time. The teas should be tested at precisely the same temperatures. The taster will take a large spoonful of tea, suck the liquid on to the taste buds all over the tongue, savour it, and spit it out. No swallowing at all.

TEA BLENDING

Once the tea is sold, the process of blending takes place after further professional tasting. One blend may be made up of different teas from Assam, Ceylon and Africa, with neutral teas added to reduce the price and round off the taste. India tea is used for its strength, Ceylon for its flavour, and African for colour, and between 10 and 40 types may be used in one blend. China teas, however, only blend well with Darjeelings and fine Ceylon teas.

Blended tea is then packaged by machine and at last delivered under its 'own label' name to the shops. The taste of a brand name has to remain constant for ever, so there has to be a certain amount of adjusting of the blend to achieve this because of the natural fluctuations in taste that occur through climatic conditions and even the time of day when harvesting takes place. The best time is said to be on a clear day, after the dew has gone and the leaves have been exposed to the sun and air for at least an hour.

SOME WELL-KNOWN TEAS

Keemun: This is the traditional tea of old Imperial China. It is grown in the north of the country and is ideal for drinking with Chinese food.

Lapsang Souchong: A large leaf China tea with a wood-smokey flavour.

Jasmine: A China tea scented with the addition of real jasmine flowers.

China Caravan: So named because of its transport from China to Russia over mountains and deserts by camel caravan.

Gunpowder: A green unfermented tea giving a very pale and thin liquor. Its name comes from its resemblance to gunpowder. It has a curled leaf and is greyish in colour.

Assam: A full-bodied tea from Assam in Northern India with a rich malty flavour.

Darjeeling: This has a muscatel flavour and comes from the foothills of the Himalayas. It is known as the champagne of teas.

Nilgiri: An Indian tea grown in the Blue Mountains of South India, light and very full of flavour.

Ceylon: Noted for its lightness, flavour and astringency.

Queen Mary: An orange pekoe from Ceylon.

English Breakfast: A blend of Indian and Ceylon teas which produces a full-bodied brew to help the British face the day.

H.M. Blend: This was originally a careful blend of several teas made for Queen Victoria.

Earl Grey: Perhaps the most famous blend of all. It was presented to the Earl by a Chinese Mandarin, and consisted of black China tea, Darjeeling and oil of bergamot.

Formosa Oolong: The most expensive tea of all, consisting of partially fermented China tea flavoured with peach blossom.

A BRIEF HISTORY OF TEA

T he legendary origin of tea is told in the story of the Chinese emperor who, 5,000 years ago, was in the habit of boiling all his drinking water. One day some leaves fell into the pot, blown by the wind, and he was so pleased with the resulting flavour that he ordered extensive planting of the tree from which the leaves had come. This was the wild tea plant.

Another story has it that when Buddha found his concentration failing during meditation, he cut off his eyelids to prevent himself from falling asleep. A tea plant sprang up fom the spot where each lid had fallen.

China was indulging in tea drinking by the sixth century and a book was produced extolling its virtues in order to help distribution and sales. Japan followed the fashion in the eighth century and evolved the elaborate Japanese tea ceremony (see page 30). Not until 1610 did any tea reach Europe, when it was brought by the Dutch from China.

The new drink reached England in 1650, to be drunk by visitors to coffee houses, in Court circles and in the upper strata of society. However, despite its price, the habit quickly spread through all classes, and by 1715 (when green tea began to be used – or *Bohea* as it was known) tea was a universal beverage.

Indian tea arrived much later, in 1838, with Ceylon tea coming in 1875.

Thomas Twining bought Tom's Coffee House in London, at the sign of the Golden Lion in the Strand, during the reign of Queen Anne (1702–14). It was in this famous meeting place of wits and bloods of the day that the word 'tip' originated. Boxes were nailed to the walls for customers to drop money into and carried a notice, '*T*o *I*nsure *P*romptness'.

Gradually, as tea became more available and popular, it was the favoured drink in all coffee houses, even being advertised as a cure-all. Its popularity led Thomas Twining to open a shop next door, the first one of its kind, for the sale of tea by weight.

Until 1784 tea was taxed in Britain at a very high rate and evasion was rife. Smuggling became a popular activity involving a wide spectrum of society, from respectable people like clergymen who put their crypts at the disposal of smugglers, to the downright dishonest and the wealthy merchants.

Dutch merchant ships brought the tea and anchored off the English coast. Small local craft then took it ashore, and underground passages leading from caves to unfrequented inland lanes provided a start to a nationwide distribution network. This profitable organisation came to an end when the tea tax was drastically reduced by William Pitt the Younger. The government then looked around for something to replace this lost revenue, and is reputed to have decided to bring in the licensing of inns and public houses . . .

The high price of tea meant that the practice of adulteration was widespread. Black tea had 'smouch' added to it, which was made from the leaf of ash trees steeped in copperas and sheep's dung. Elder buds were mixed with green tea. Penalties were imposed but failed to check this profiteering as tea was sold loose by grocers.

In 1826 John Horniman acted for the benefit of the public and set up a small business in the Isle of Wight where he put unadulterated tea into sealed paper packets with a guaranteed net weight. The public reacted with enthusiasm and the system became general practice.

———————◆———————

'Tea, though ridiculed by those who are naturally coarse in their nervous sensibilities . . . will always be the favoured beverage of the intellectual.'

Thomas de Quincey (1795–1859)

THE BOSTON TEA PARTY

The Boston Tea Party is one of those historical episodes which people have heard of and yet have often forgotten its origins. It can be regarded as the trigger that set off the American War of Independence (1775–83).

Colonists had brought tea to the New World, where it quickly became as popular as it was back home. When Parliament began to tax the American colonies without the consent of their assemblies, tea was one of the items they selected. The colonists refused to pay and began to trade in smuggled tea from Holland.

The East India Company, who had the monopoly for importing and exporting tea, were thus faced with the loss of a main market and an embarrassing stock of millions of pounds in weight of tea. In 1773, therefore, the Company persuaded Parliament to pass the Tea Act which gave them the right to export tea from China direct to America. This cut out both the London and the American importers.

The colonists refused to pay the tax. They joined with the American importers in an angry reaction which ended in the event we now know as the Boston Tea Party. Under the cover of darkness, 50 men disguised as Red Indians boarded British ships in the harbour at Boston and tossed £10,000's worth of tea overboard. Other ports followed suit, and an outraged British Parliament retaliated with strong measures which resulted in war. Hardly a storm in a teacup!

TEA CLIPPERS

The era of the tea clippers can be said to have evolved from the American War of Independence, for these three-masted, fully rigged ships developed from the privateers built in Baltimore as part of the fighting force against the British. Much later, in 1850, the first British clipper named *Stornaway* was built in Aberdeen. It was to be the first of some 26 tea clippers built in Britain, of which the *Taeping* was one of the most famous and the *Cutty Sark* one of the last.

Annual clipper races were held, which created vast public interest as a sporting event. The ships would load their cargo of tea in China and leave Foochow on the same tide, sail down the China Sea, across the Indian Ocean, round the Cape and up the Atlantic coast, past the Azores and into the English Channel. The race actually finished with tugs towing the ships up the Thames to the Port of London and the throwing ashore of the chests of tea. The winning merchant gained a premium of 6d a pound at auction and there was a high cash award to both captain and crew. The last clipper race took place in 1866.

After the opening of the Suez Canal in 1869 steam began to take over from sail and the clippers were forced to give up their service to tea and turn to the longer Australian wool run.

TEA AND SCOTLAND

The return in 1680 of the exiled Duke and Duchess of York (later James II of England and VII of Scotland) from The Hague brought the fashion for tea drinking to Holyrood House in Edinburgh. Before long the new beverage was being drunk throughout the land.

The first sales of tea in Scotland were made by a jeweller called George Smith from his Edinburgh shop. His theory was that the value of precious stones and metals would enhance the value of tea if they were sold side by side. When health-giving properties began to be attributed to tea (see page 21), apothecaries sold it with enthusiasm. There was also a practice in Scotland of brewing tea and storing it in barrels, to be served out like beer!

Ceylon suffered some disastrous coffee crop failures during the nineteenth century and Scottish pioneers were responsible for trying a changeover to tea planting. Their complete success has left a legacy of tea garden names throughout the island, names such as Barra, Culloden, Gleneagles and Strathspey. In addition, all engineers working in the factories of tea gardens are called Mac, in the same way that ships' engineers are Macs because so many of them are Scots.

During the long period of high taxation on tea, smuggling became as much a necessity in Scotland, as it was in England. In this case the more northern ports of Scandinavia were the sources of contraband tea.

The Scots went on to play a major part in the 10-year campaign by the tea trade to overthrow the East India Company's monopoly and allow other operators to bring tea into Britain. The campaign was led by William Thorburn and a group of Edinburgh tea merchants. A Scot, Kirkman Finlay of Glasgow, made history when he commissioned the *Buckinghamshire* to sail direct from Calcutta to

Glasgow in defiance of the monopoly. Success came in 1834 when the government did not renew the East India Company's charter.

The famous name of Thomas Lipton was that of a young Scot who opened a provision shop in Glasgow in 1876, the first of a string of shops throughout Britain that sold his tea.

THE PRICE OF TEA

At the time when tea became such a popular drink in Britain, a worker would have had to spend a third of his weekly wage to buy a pound of tea, and it would seem that he did this willingly.

Nowadays a ¼ lb of tea can cost as much as 60p for regular brands. The most expensive is Formosa Oolong with its peach blossom aroma which costs approximately £14 per lb. The following table shows the fluctuating cost of tea through the centuries:

1657	16/- to 60/- per lb
1700	10/- to 36/- per lb
1756	10/- to 12/- per lb
1784	16/- to 50/- per lb
1839	6/6d per lb
1870	3/- per lb
1910	3/- per lb

TEA AND HEALTH

For 500 years China tea was considered a medicine by the Japanese, to whom it was introduced in AD 800. But when tea was first introduced into Europe it was looked upon with suspicion by the medical profession. Some doctors denounced the new beverage as pernicious to health, an obstruction to industry, and an impoverishment to the nation. But gradually opinion changed, with a Dr Cornelius Bontekoe in Holland recommending the use of up to 10 cups a day, and even as many as 50 or 100 – he claimed to drink as many himself.

When apothecaries in Scotland started to sell tea, this was also a boost to sales. Traces of this custom remain in the names of some of today's popular brands. *Typhoo*, for instance, is Chinese for doctor; *P.G. Tips* meant pre-gestive tips; and *99 Tea* was known as *Doctor's* or *Prescription* tea because that was the number on old prescription forms.

Four important constituents of tea are caffeine, theophylline, theobr∩mine, and polyphenols.

Caffeine stimulates the central nervous system and respiration and also influences the metabolic processes of all body cells. Indian tea contains more caffeine than China tea, and tea only has a third the amount of caffeine compared with coffee. The immediate effect of a cup of tea is its comforting warmth; it takes several minutes for the caffeine to be felt.

Theophylline and theobromine act similarly but in a milder manner, and also help muscle relaxation.

Polyphenols, or tannin, give the taste to tea, but over-infusion should be avoided in order not to upset the proper balance. Again, Indian tea contains more tannin than China.

Tea on its own contains no calories. However, with milk and sugar added it can provide 40 to 50 calories a cup. Tea contains several of the B complex vitamins, so if you were to drink 6 cups of tea a day, that would provide about 10 per cent of the average adult's daily requirement.

The Chinese are very good with preventative medicine and are said only to pay their doctors while remaining fit. So it may be worthwhile following their custom of stuffing a pillow with dry tea leaves, which they say is beneficial for the eyes.

TEA AND FAMOUS CHARACTERS

*Queen Anne enjoyed tea and did much to popularize it. Alexander Pope wrote of her in *The Rape of the Lock*:

'Here thou, great Anna, whom three realms obey,
Dost sometimes counsel take – and sometimes tay.'

* Lord Nelson and the Duke of Wellington always made sure they had supplies of tea handy during their battles with Napoleon. The Duke had a special silver teapot that went everywhere with him.

* Emma Hart was referred to as 'the fair tea-maker of Edgware Road' by Sir William Hamilton before she became his wife.

* Pity the Duke of Argyll who returned from the East with what he thought was the tea plant, hoping to cultivate it, then found that it was *Lycium Chinensis*, a plant which can now be found in hedgerows.

* Gladstone would fill his stone hot water bottle with tea so that he could have a drink to hand during the night.

* Dr Johnson described himself as:

    'A hardened and shameless tea-drinker, who has for twenty years diluted his meals with only the infusion of this fascinating plant; whose kettle has scarcely time to cool; who with tea amuses the evening, with tea solaces the midnight, and with tea welcomes the morning.'

* Dr Johnson to Mrs Thrale:

    And now, I pray thee, Hetty dear,
    That thou wilt give to me,
    With cream and sugar soften'd well
    Another dish of tea.

    But hear, alas! this mournful truth,
    Nor hear it with a frown, –
    Thou canst not make the tea so fast
    As I can gulp it down.

TIME FOR TEA

AFTERNOON TEA

Anna, Duchess of Bedford, originated the British custom of taking afternoon tea in about 1840. She used to feel hungry during the hours between three and five o'clock and she introduced the habit of taking a drink of tea at that time. The habit spread, as did the quantity of bread or cake eaten with it.

'There are few hours in life more agreeable than the hour dedicated to the ceremony known as afternoon tea.'

Henry James (1843–1916)

TEA BREAKS

During the Industrial Revolution attempts were made to stop factory workers from drinking tea on the grounds that it was not good for the working classes and made them 'lazy and idle and prone to slothfulness'. The prohibition had no success, and today most organisations allow for official tea breaks.

> Oh, the fact'ries may be roaring
> With a boom-a-lack, zoom-a-lack-a whee!
> But there isn't any roar
> When the clock strikes four,
> Everything stops for tea.
>
> Oh, a lawyer in a court-room
> In the middle of an alimony plea
> Has to stop and help 'em pour
> When the clock strikes four,
> Everything stops for tea.
>
> Now I know just why Franz Schubert
> Didn't finish his Unfinished Symphony
> He might have written more
> But the clock struck four,
> Everything stops for tea.

Verses from 'Everything Stops for Tea' written by Zigler, Goodheart and Hoffman
Reproduced by kind permission of Cinephonic Music Co. Ltd

TEA GARDENS

Tea plantations are referred to as tea gardens, but in the middle of the eighteenth century, when the popularity of the traditional coffee houses was waning, out-of-town places of entertainment began to develop. These too were called tea gardens and they provided opportunities for all the family to enjoy themselves. Londoners flocked to the gardens at Vauxhall, Ranelagh and Marylebone. Soon everyone from the elite to the apprentices and tradesmen frequented these pleasant gardens where illuminations and fireworks added to the attractions.

Unfortunately, progress overtook the gardens as London spread outwards. By the start of the 19th century outdoor entertainment lost its popularity. The next drinking spots for tea became the teashops.

TEASHOPS AND TEAROOMS

Until the opening of the first Aerated Bread Company's teashops in 1880 there was nowhere a lady could have a meal by herself in safety and respectability. This chain of shops grew during that decade and was followed in 1894 by the first Lyons' teashop in Piccadilly. Gunter's was already established as a high-class place in which to sip tea and sample delicate cakes, when an American lady called Mrs Fuller expressed concern at the lack of sufficient places for refreshment where ladies of the leisured class could congregate. She set up the first of the many shops that carried her name well into this century.

The need for teashops increased as train services began to offer the chance of spending a day in the large London department stores. Ladies from the provinces took advantage of this facility and the stores realised the advantage of providing tearooms themselves. They added a ladies' orchestra for background music. It was all most elegant and soothing, particularly at Whiteley's where one could sit at tea and look over the gallery rails down the well of the central marble staircase modelled on the stairway at La Scala, Milan.

TEAGOWNS

The influence of the Aesthetic Movement which encouraged the making of looser garments for entertaining at home, and the softer fabrics being offered by Liberty's, gave rise to the fashion for teagowns in the early 1900s. This had a long and romantic reign, and shops like Woolands, Marshall and Snellgrove, and the Army and Navy Stores became famous for their gowns trimmed with embroidery, cascading lace and pleated frills.

NURSERY TEA

Unlike today's child who rushes in from school and helps itself from the fridge, children brought up under a Victorian influence would have nursery tea. The strict eye of Nanny would watch that proper manners were exercised and all rules obeyed. 'Now, Master Tommy, just you eat up your brown bread.

Then you may have two slices of white, and *then*, if you're good, a slice of cake.'

A relaxation of this routine was allowed in my father's nursery days whenever there was a birthday. He and his sisters were allowed to eat what they liked on such a day, and also to behave as they wished at the table. Their favourite ploy was to try making maps of the world by spilling tea on to the tablecloth. Even fun, it seems, had to be edifying.

VILLAGE TEAS

If you are ever faced with the daunting prospect of providing tea for the village fête, you may find it helpful to follow these measures:

1 lb of tea will make 80 single teapots.
1 lb of tea bags will give 112 single cups.
Allow 2 cubes of sugar per person and 3 teaspoons of milk.

JAPANESE TEA CEREMONY

'A estheticism of austere simplicity and refined poverty' is one definition of the spirit of *chanoyu*, the Japanese tea ceremony. It features the serving and drinking of a powdered thick green tea called *matcha* in special surroundings and with traditional rules and utensils. Its codes of behaviour have been set down under the influence of Zen Buddhism. I give here a very brief summary of a custom which often puzzles Westerners, who might well benefit from something similar to relax them from the stresses and strains of everyday life.

A typical *chanoyu* party consists of a host and five guests and takes place in a *sukiya*, tea house. This contains a tea room, preparation room, waiting room, and an inner garden. It is built in a secluded part of the main garden and is reached along a special path. The participants, male or female, wear silk kimonos and traditional white socks. Each guest brings a small folding fan and a pad of *kaishi*, little paper napkins.

There are four parts to the ceremony which takes four hours. First a light meal is served, followed by a short recess, and then the main part of the ceremony when a thick tea is offered, and finally the serving of *usucha* which is a thin textured tea. This last service is often performed on its own and takes only an hour.

The ritual begins with the host leading the guests to the tea house along the special path, stopping on the way to wash hands and rinse out the mouth in a stone basin. They then crawl through the low doorway of the tea room, thereby humbling themselves, before kneeling to admire, from behind the respectfully held fans, a hanging scroll in an alcove. After observing the hearth or brazier that heats the water they all take their places for the meal. At its conclusion the host invites the guests to retire to the waiting room or to a bench in the inner garden.

The main ceremony is heralded by the striking of a gong. When the guests re-enter, after further purification, they find the scroll replaced by a vase of flowers, and the tea-making requisites laid out. These consist of the tea bowl, tea container, and bamboo tea whisk and scoop. The host performs a ritual cleansing of the utensils before putting three scoopfuls of *matcha* per guest into a bowl, mixes it with a ladleful of hot water and whips the mixture until it is like thick green pea soup. This tea is made from the young leaves of plants that are 20 to 70 years old. The principal guest now moves on his knees to pick up the bowl, bow to the others, and sip while balancing the bowl on the palm of the left hand

and supporting it on one side with the fingers of the other hand. The taste is praised, two more sips taken, and the rim where the lips touched wiped with the paper napkin before the bowl is passed to the next guest.

The last part of the ceremony is the serving of *usucha*, the lighter version of tea which is made from plants under 15 years old. Another difference is that the tea is made individually for each person with two or two and a half scoops of tea, and all the liquid has to be drunk. This time the rim of the bowl is cleaned with the fingers of the right hand and the fingers themselves wiped with the napkin.

After the host has carried the utensils out of the room he makes a silent bow to denote that the ceremony is over, before leading the way out of the tea house.

ICED TEAS

An Englishman called Richard Blechynden 'discovered' iced tea in 1904 when he was trying to sell cups of hot tea to the public at the World Fair in St Louis. No one was interested as there was a heatwave on at the time. In desperation he added ice cubes! Here is how to make iced tea in the proper way:

Fill a glass jug with cold water and add 2 tea bags for each pint. Cover the jug and store in the fridge for at least 8 hours or overnight. Using cold water produces a clear amber tea liquor and prevents an acid taste. But if you use hot water and let the tea cool, the liquor becomes cloudy as it cools due to the action of the caffeine and other constituents which form a natural 'cream' or precipitate in the tea.

RUSSIAN ROULETTE: Put ice in a glass. Add a double measure of vodka and a single measure of lime juice. Top up with iced tea as desired.

APPLE APERITIF: Add 1 pint of carbonated clear apple juice and a wine glass of clear lemon juice to 1 pint of iced tea.

TEA PLANTER'S PUNCH: Add 1 wine glass of brandy to the recipe for *Apple Aperitif*.

TEA FIZZ: Add 1 pint of lemonade and a wine glass of lime juice to 1 pint of iced tea. Stir with ice.

TO MAKE A GOOD POT OF TEA

Fill the kettle with fresh cold water from the mains tap if possible. Warm the teapot by rinsing it out with hot water or, better still, by standing it near heat. Add one teaspoon of tea per person and perhaps one for the pot. As soon as the water boils pour it on to the leaves. Always take the pot to the kettle to catch the very moment of boiling because over-boiled water produces a bitter and muddy brew due to oxygen loss. Leave the tea to infuse for five minutes, then give a good stir. Some experts recommend stirring immediately after the boiling water is added.

The water in some districts makes a better brew than in others, but one usually becomes used to whatever is on tap. Hard water can make the tea cloudy with a thin surface skin to it. Naturally soft water produces a good golden colour, but artificially softened water will spoil the taste and make for a muddy result. Filtered water produces a very good cup of tea.

MILK OR LEMON?

Continentals and slimmers prefer to add lemon to their tea, but in Britain milk is more common. If milk is put in after the tea there is a belief that the drinker will remain a bachelor. The custom of using milk came from France in about 1680 from the inspiration of a courtesan who had a sick friend who was ordered to drink milk to make her better. As she hated milk, the courtesan suggested that it should be added to her favourite drink, tea.

A more downright and practical reason for the addition of milk, and for putting it in first, was the protection of fine bone china cups. The cold milk would prevent cracking when the very hot liquid was poured in.

It is best to leave out the milk when making tea in a thermos. A kind of caramel flavour often develops.

SUGAR

This is entirely a question of taste, though a purist will quail at the thought of thus masking the pure flavour of tea. It should be remembered that a cup of tea with lemon and no milk or sugar contains no calories.

'Love and scandal are the best sweeteners of tea.'

Henry Fielding (1707–54)

Storage Of Tea

Tea easily absorbs moisture and odours and so it is essential to keep it in a dry place away from any strong smelling items. An airtight tin is best or any type of proper caddy. This word caddy is derived from *catty* which was the name of an Oriental measure of weight.

The expensive tea that was first used in British households was usually kept in caddies with locks, required quantities being doled out to the servants only as required. Caddies were made of silver, jasper, ivory, earthenware and wood, and the tea was often blended at table by the mistress of the house from a caddy that contained compartments for the different types of tea and a bowl for mixing.

* If through incautious storage near strong smelling foods tea becomes contaminated, there is no need for despair. Spread the tea on to a sheet of paper in a fresh atmosphere for a few hours and it will breathe out any flavour it has breathed in.

* If a teapot becomes stale and smelly it will be sweetened by leaving some dry tea in it for several days.

When the Chinese realised that they could keep tea for longer periods if they dried their green tea, they looked for an economical method of fuelling the drying method. They burned old ropes. (Wood is now preferred.)

It is reassuring to know that in these days of butter mountains and milk lakes, tea is never stockpiled. Flavour is too precious to be treated in this manner.

TEAPOTS

The best tea is made in glazed china and earthenware pots. Silver teapots also produce a good brew but are, of course, expensive and a bore to keep clean. Stainless steel pots work well as they stand up to hard wear, but if enamelled ware is used care must be taken to see that the enamel is not chipped inside.

The traditional shape for a teapot is round, but collectors will find a wealth of different shapes and sizes – from shapes like cabbages and cottages to all kinds of animal shapes.

The biggest teapot in the world was featured at the Great Exhibition of 1851. It held 13½ gallons and stood two and a half feet high.

COSIES

A padded cosy is used to hold in the heat – one might look upon a cosy as a tea duvet. Shapes include crinoline ladies, beehives, country cottages, cats, almost anything that ingenuity can dream up. They may be made of patchwork, elaborate quilting or plain materials, be covered in embroidery, beading, or lace. Some may even have removable loose covers. There used to be rather ugly metal cosies that were hinged and lined with felt.

People who take their tea very seriously do not advocate the use of cosies because they cause the contents of such a pampered pot to stew, and that ruins the flavour.

TEACUPS

Early teacups were imported from China and had no handles. When home production of cups in Britain began to develop these were also made without handles. They were smaller than the cups of today because tea was expensive and had to be eked out.

Making tea ware was the basis for the English pottery and porcelain industry located in the Midlands, soon to become known as the Potteries. Cups of every pattern imaginable, now with handles, and in larger sizes, were manufactured. A really quirky shape was the moustache cup which had a small ledge inside the brim on which a gentleman's whiskers could rest without getting wet!

Before carrying a full cup of tea, give it a good stir. This will prevent any of it slopping over into the saucer.

STRAINERS

The most practical strainer is the type that is held over the cup as the tea is poured from the pot. Most teapots have an inbuilt ledge with perforations incorporated at the base of the spout which effectively holds back most of the leaves, and of course the use of the teabag does away with the need for straining devices altogether.

There used to be a type of tea strainer that consisted of a small dangling metal basket with flexible arms which were inserted into the spout. The idea was that the basket swung into position to catch the liquid as it was poured. A certain degree of faith was required, plus non-hesitant action.

TEA BAGS

One story has it that the first tea bag was invented by accident when a Chinese tea merchant sent his sample to London packed in little silk bags. Another, that a New York wholesaler, Thomas Sullivan, was responsible. He also sent samples of tea to his customers in small silk bags. The modern tea bag is now used all over the world, and the type of tea used is one of the smallest leaf, such as Fannings or Dust.

A tea bag is very often used to make a mug of tea, in much the same way that one used to use a metal infuser – which was like two perforated teaspoons clamped together. However, some care is needed even for making tea with tea bags. The mug should first be warmed, and the tea bag allowed to infuse for two to three minutes in order to obtain good flavour and not just coloured water. The mug should be covered during infusion to keep in the heat. Remember, a tea bag is not instant tea.

TINNED TEA AND OTHERS

To purists, the very idea of tinned or bottled tea sounds like heresy, but these products, which are carbonated, make an excellent and cooling drink which is popular in Sri Lanka, Indonesia and some other parts of the world. It is quite likely that one day they will arrive in Europe to join the ranks of the many tinned and bottled drinks already on sale.

Instant tea has been available for some time, usually flavoured with lemon, and in the catering world there is something called liquid tea, which is a frozen product.

WAKE UP!

An automatic teamaker is as popular a retirement present as the ubiquitous gold watch. The invention is not a recent one. An early example, produced in 1902, was advertised as 'The clock that makes tea'. It was a real Heath Robinson affair and consisted of an alarm clock, copper kettle, spirit lamp, and various springs that activated the process. Ignition came from the drawing of an ordinary match across sandpaper. After the boiling water was poured into the pot from the tilted kettle, the alarm rang for a second time to announce that all was ready. The contraption retailed at prices from 25/- to 70/-. An example can be seen in the Domestic Appliances Gallery at the Science Museum in London.

SUPERSTITIONS

* If two people pour from the same pot it is believed that the second runs the risk of giving birth to a red headed child before the year is up.

* Stirring the tea in the pot will stir up trouble. Small wonder there is so much trouble in the world!

* Bubbles that rise and collect on the surface of tea in the cup are a promise of money to come.

* Small sticks of tea which float to the top of the cup signal the approach of visiting strangers. If thin a lady may be expected, and if fat a gentleman. The stick should be fished out and placed on the back of the left hand and the left wrist struck sharply with the side of the other hand. The number of blows it takes to dislodge the stick corresponds to the number of the days before the visit.

* Here is another version. Fish out your stranger and place him (or her) on the back of your left hand. Clench your right hand and bring the side of your fist down on the stranger. If it sticks first time, then the stranger will appear today. If it doesn't, try again for tomorrow, the next day, and so on. Once your stranger has stuck to the side of your right hand press it against your forehead. If it sticks, then the stranger will kiss you!

FORTUNE TELLING

R eading the tea leaves in a drained cup is a comprehensive method of divination, particularly with a skilled interpreter. Briefly, the rules are as follows:

The inquirer should drink from the cup until only a teaspoonful of liquid remains. Swirl this three times round in an anti-clockwise direction while concentrating on the question needing a solution. Next invert the cup on to the saucer and leave for a few moments.

Now the interpretation begins. Take the cup in both hands, remembering that the handle represents the inquirer. Leaves close to the brim relate to events soon to occur and those at the bottom of the cup to bad tidings. Close to the handle they concern matters at home. Scattered dots around the cup mean the prospect of financial gain, straight lines indicate progress, and circles completion.

Here is a short list of shapes and their interpretation, but it must be remembered that a symbol or pattern may have its meaning altered by others nearby. So all symbols should be read in conjunction with each other.

Symbol	*Meaning*
Aeroplane	Promotion
Anchor	Success
Bird	Positive omen, especially when on right or near handle

Cross	Trouble
Face	Change
Key	Improved business, but robbery if at bottom of cup
Ladder	Advancement
Letter M	Someone does not have your best interests at heart
Umbrella	Shelter
Ring	Marriage
Ship	Travel
Star	Good fortune
Triangle	Inheritance
Wings	Messages
Windmill	Success through hard work

OTHER USES FOR TEA

* An old-fashioned cure for tired eyes was to bathe them in an eye bath of cold tea. Now a cold, used tea bag is more likely to be employed on the closed eyelids while resting.

* An infusion of China tea and a heaped teaspoon of dried sage used when cool as a final hair rinse helps to lessen the effect of greying.

* Lace can be successfully and safely dyed by soaking in warm tea. Faded net curtains or stockings also benefit from this treatment, but it has to be repeated after every wash.

* Theatre directors who do not want to have their actors falling about drunk and forgetting their words on stage, provide them with cold tea in decanters when whisky is called for in the script.

* Hot sweet tea used to be the top first aid treatment for shock, but it is now going out of favour. However, a cup of tea is always the first remedy one thinks of in home crises.

* When a saucepan burns, the best way to remove the black crust is to pour into it leftover tea, possibly with the addition of some salt, and leave for at least 24 hours.

* Soothe tired feet by soaking in a bowl of cold tea to which has been added the juice of 1 lemon and a pinch of salt.

* In the garden it makes sense that camellias enjoy the dregs of the teapot tipped out round their roots. The camellia is the shrub that in the right climate and with the right care gives us tea to drink. Many indoor plants also enjoy a cup of char.

* Varnished woodwork can be successfully cleaned with a solution of strong cold tea.

TEA RECIPES

KASHMIR SOUP

Guests who are served this lovely soup are always mystified when they try to guess the ingredients – a good talking point to start off the meal.

8 oz dark dried apricots
1 pint cold tea
1 pint chicken stock
handful of chopped mint
pinch of garam masala or curry powder
salt and pepper
1/4 pint double cream
3 fl oz medium dry sherry
mint leaves to garnish

Rinse apricots and soak overnight in cold tea.

Next day put apricots and tea into a pan and simmer till tender. Purée apricots and any remaining tea in a blender. Pour into a large pan and stir in stock, mint, garam masala or curry powder, salt and pepper. Stir in cream and sherry. Thin if necessary with extra chicken stock. Reheat.

Garnish with mint leaves before serving.

Serves 4–6

BREWED LAMB CASSEROLE

An unusual but very simple lamb casserole. Delicious with boiled or baked potatoes.

1 shank end leg lamb, cut into cubes
2 medium onions, sliced
1 tablespoon seasoned flour
1 tablespoon mixed herbs
1½ pints Twinings Darjeeling tea
small packet frozen peas
small can sweetcorn
cream to serve (optional)

Lightly brown the cubes of lamb on all sides in its own fat. Add onions and brown. Sprinkle with seasoned flour and herbs and cook on a low heat for 1 or 2 minutes, stirring. Stir in tea and bring to the boil.

Cover and simmer for 1¾ hours. Add peas and sweetcorn. Heat for 10 minutes more, then check seasoning and serve with a swirl of cream.

Serves 4

HAM ROAST WITH SPICED TEA GLAZE

A marvellous dish if you've got lots of hungry people to feed.

large gammon joint, at least 5 lbs
1 tablespoon Twinings Jasmine tea from the packet
¼ pint boiling water
8 oz can pineapple rings, cut in pieces
2 oz maraschino cherries, chopped
1 tablespoon cornflour

Put the gammon in a pan of cold water and slowly bring to the boil. Simmer very gently, allowing 20 minutes to the 1 lb. Remove gammon 1½ hours before it is completely cooked.

Steep the tea in boiling water for 5 minutes, then strain. In a pan, mix the tea, pineapple pieces, cherries and cornflour and cook over a low heat, stirring constantly until the glaze thickens. Spoon one third of the glaze over the partially cooked ham.

Roast the ham at 180°C, 350°F, Gas 4 for 30 minutes. Spoon one third more of the glaze over ham. Return to oven and bake another 30 minutes. Repeat with final one third of glaze and roast for 30 minutes more.

Cut ham in thin slices and top each with some of the pan juices.

Serves about 12

STEAMED SAVOURY RICE

1/2 oz margarine
1 onion, diced
8 oz long grain rice
1 teaspoon each turmeric and mixed herbs
1 pint Earl Grey tea
1/2 teaspoon salt

Melt the margarine in a pan and sauté the onion and rice for about 5 minutes. Add turmeric and herbs. Stir well, then add the tea and salt. Cover with tightly fitting lid and steam on the lowest heat possible until the rice is cooked but still a little firm.

Serves 4

SPICED SALAD DRESSING

Very good mixed with ham or chicken pieces, and also with fruit compote.

3 tea bags and 1/2 cup of boiling water
1 cup plain yoghurt
1/4 cup honey
1 teaspoon grated lemon rind
1 tablespoon lemon juice

Steep tea for 5 minutes in the boiling water. Strain and leave to cool.
   Place yoghurt in a bowl and stir in tea, honey, lemon rind and juice. Chill.

Sweet Pancakes

The use of tea instead of milk imparts a more robust quality to the pancakes, suitable for sweet fillings.

4 oz plain flour
pinch of salt
1 egg
1/2 pint of cold prepared tea
oil for frying

Sift the flour and salt into a large bowl. Make a central depression in the mound of flour with the 'pointed' end of the egg before breaking it into the well it has formed. Gradually incorporate the flour into the egg, adding tea by degrees and beating well.

Heat a minimum amount of oil in a frying pan over a high heat and pour in about 2 tablespoons of batter to make pancakes in the usual way. Fill with jam, stewed fruit, etc.

Makes 10

Dried Fruit Compote

Cooking dried fruit in tea instead of water produces a richer flavour both in the fruit and the juice.

12 oz mixed dried fruit (apricots, peaches, apple rings, prunes, sultanas)
2 pints freshly made tea
3 tablespoons sugar

2 teaspoons grated orange rind
juice of 1 lemon

Wash the fruit and put in a baking dish with the hot tea. Cover and bake for about 1 hour at 140°C, 275°F, Gas 1, until the fruit is plump and soft but still whole.

Pour off the juices into a pan. Add sugar, orange rind and lemon juice. Stir and simmer for 5 minutes. Pour this syrup over the fruit. Chill.

Serves 4

TEA JELLY

Substituting tea for plain water gives a children's party jelly a much more sophisticated taste.

1 lemon jelly
1¾ cups freshly made black tea
grated rind of 2 fresh lemons

To decorate:
lemon slices
whipped cream

Dissolve jelly in half of the hot tea. When it starts to thicken, add the grated lemon rind and the rest of the tea. Pour into wetted moulds. Leave to set, then chill. Turn out and decorate with lemon butterflies and whipped cream.

Serves 4

FROZEN APRICOT TEA MOUSSE

Slowly, the nutrition experts are educating us to eat more wisely and not to indulge in sugar and cream. But when a special occasion warrants a particularly naughty extravagance, why not serve this confection which carries a definite taste of tea.

1 envelope (0.4 oz/11 g) gelatine
4 tablespoons cold water
4 oz sugar
½ pint hot double strength Twinings Earl Grey or Assam tea
lemon juice to taste
1 pint whipped double cream
1 lb can apricot halves, drained and diced

Sprinkle gelatine over the water and stir over a low heat till dissolved.

Mix sugar and hot tea in a bowl. Stir in lemon juice to taste and the dissolved gelatine. Continue to stir until slightly thickened. Fold in whipped cream and apricots. Pour mixture into a freezer container, cover and freeze until hard.

To serve, scoop or spoon into cold serving dishes.

Serves 8

Oat And Coconut Biscuits

1 rounded tablespoon syrup
5 oz butter or margarine
4 oz caster sugar
3 oz porridge oats
2 oz desiccated coconut
4 oz plain flour, sieved
2 level tablespoons bicarbonate of soda
2 tablespoons hot tea

Place syrup, butter and sugar in a pan and heat gently until melted. Mix oats, coconut and sieved flour together and add to melted mixture. Dissolve bicarbonate of soda in hot tea and add to mixture. Mix well and cool.

Roll mixture into balls the size of a walnut. Place on a greased baking sheet, well apart. Bake at 160°C, 325°F, Gas 3 for 12–15 minutes. Cool slightly before removing from baking tray.

Makes about 40 biscuits

CRUMBLE DATE COOKIES

8 oz plain flour
good pinch of salt
3 oz caster sugar
4 oz porridge oats
5 oz butter or margarine, melted
6 oz dates, chopped
1 oz walnuts, chopped
¼ pint tea

Sieve flour and salt into a basin. Add sugar and oats. Bind with melted butter to form crumbly mixture.

Put dates, walnuts and tea into a pan and cook for a few minutes until softened.

Put half of crumble mixture into base of a swiss roll tin 12 × 8 inches. Cover with date mixture and top with rest of crumble. Press down well. Bake at 180°C, 350°F, Gas 4 for 55–60 minutes.

Cut into 20 squares.

TEA SCONES

8 oz self-raising flour
¼ teaspoon salt
1 oz sugar
1 oz butter
¼ pint strong cold tea
4 oz sultanas

Mix flour, salt and sugar in a bowl. Rub in the butter, then add the tea and sultanas. Mix into a soft handling dough.

Shape into a round on greased and floured baking sheet. Mark into triangles. Bake at 190°C, 375°F, Gas 5 for about 20 minutes.

COUNTRY TEA BREAD

This keeps in an airtight tin for up to three weeks.

8 oz mixed dried fruit
1/4 pint English Breakfast tea
4 tablespoons clear honey
1 beaten egg
8 oz self-raising flour, sieved
pinch of salt
1 oz butter, melted

Topping:
1 tablespoon honey
1 oz demerara sugar
1 oz chopped walnuts

Put fruit, tea and honey in a bowl. Cover and leave overnight.

Next day, stir in beaten egg, sifted flour, salt and melted butter. Transfer to a greased 1 lb bread tin.

Bake at 180°C, 350°F, Gas 4 for about 50 minutes. Take out of the oven, brush bread with honey, and sprinkle sugar and walnuts on top. Bake for another 20 minutes. Slice and serve with butter.

APPLE AND DATE TEA CHUTNEY

4 lb cooking apples
1½ lb onions
2 garlic cloves, chopped
8 oz stoned dates
½ pint strong tea
1½ pints malt vinegar
1½ lb granulated sugar
4 teaspoons salt
3 teaspoons ground ginger
1 tablespoon pickling spice, tied in muslin

Peel, core and slice the apples. Peel the onions and chop roughly. Coarsely mince the apples, onions, garlic and dates. Put in a large pan, add tea and bring to the boil. Cover and simmer for 30 minutes.

Add the remaining ingredients, except the pickling spice, to the apple mixture and stir over a low heat until the sugar has dissolved.

Add the spice bag and bring the mixture to the boil. Lower the heat and simmer uncovered until the chutney is the consistency of jam and a dark brown. This will take 2 to 3 hours. Cool in the pan before putting into jars.

Makes about 4 pounds

TISANES

T isanes go way back into folklore and were used as hot infusions for medicinal reasons, and even as aphrodisiacs. Many herbs are used and they may be mixed with ordinary tea.

BORAGE

To make: 1 tablespoon of chopped leaves
1 cup of boiling water
Infuse for 5 minutes.

To use: Rich in calcium and potassium. The 17th-century diarist John Evelyn recommended it for 'cheering the hard student'. It has a taste of cucumber.

CHAMOMILE

To make: 1 teaspoon of dried flowers
1 cup of boiling water
Infuse for 3 minutes.

To use: Good as a nightcap. Also prevents indigestion and soothes sunburn.

LIME

To make: 1 teaspoon of flowers
½ pint of water
Boil together for 5 minutes and strain.

To use: For nerves, catarrh, insomnia and coughs.

MATTE

This Paraguayan herb tea is bought ready-made and can be successfully mixed with ordinary tea in a proportion of 1 to 3. The flavour is excellent, and lemon may be added. It is claimed to aid clear thought – so, again, good for students.

NETTLE

To make: 1 ounce of nettle tops
1 pint of boiling water
Infuse briefly, strain thoroughly, and drink while hot.

To use: Helps to relieve arthritic and rheumatic pain.

PEPPERMINT

To make: A handful of fresh leaves
2 cups of boiling water
Infuse for 5 minutes.

To use: Wards off colds, relieves headaches and aids digestion.

SAGE

To make: 1 tablespoon of coarsely chopped leaves
1 cup of boiling water
Infuse for 5 minutes.

To use: Leaves the mouth fresh and clean. Reduces inflammation, suppresses perspiration and allays shock. It was once so popular in China that traders would trade 4 pounds of ordinary tea for 1 of English sage.

VALERIAN

To make: ¼ ounce of leaves
¼ pint of cold water
Leave to draw for 12 hours. Strain.

To use: A mild sedative.

Now stir the fire, and close the shutters fast.
Let fall the curtains, wheel the sofa round,
And, while the bubbling and loud hissing urn
Throws up a steady column, and the cups
That cheer, but do not inebriate, wait on each,
So, let us welcome peaceful evening in.

William Cowper (1731–1800)

Acknowledgements

Thanks are due to The Tea Council, Science Museum, Twinings, The Japanese Embassy, E.M.I. Publishing and Campbell Connelly for the help so freely given.